# The Road to the ✝ Leads Home

A Poetic Invitation

FAYE STEWART

WESTBOW
PRESS®
A DIVISION OF THOMAS NELSON
& ZONDERVAN

WestBow Press books may be ordered through
booksellers or by contacting:

WestBow Press
A Division of Thomas Nelson & Zondervan
1663 Liberty Drive
Bloomington, IN 47403
www.westbowpress.com
1 (866) 928-1240

ISBN: 978-1-4908-9954-1 (sc)
ISBN: 978-1-4908-9955-8 (e)

Library of Congress Control Number: 2015918031

Print information available on the last page.

WestBow Press rev. date: 02/25/2016

You're Invited:

Place:    Home

Date:    Now is the time

RSVP:    JESUS @ 1-800-HELP 4 ME!

\* \* \* \* \* \* \*

## Dedication

To Mom, who always believed "anything
I wrote was special."

# Acknowledgement

Thank you to my friend Bonnie Abernathy who encouraged me to share these thoughts with others and to take a step of faith into publishing. Your love for God's Word, vision for this project, and support have been invaluable.

# Contents

Introduction ................................................................. xiii

An Invitation from Christ ................................................. 1

His Invitation to Me ...................................................... 13

His Invitation to Individuals ...........................................31

His Invitation to the World.............................................43

Your Reply to His Invitation ......................................... 53

Benediction................................................................. 67

# Introduction

An invitation for me?
Who is it from?
Jesus ... wants to see me?

The meeting place: Here?
- Is that a knock at the door?
- Should I answer?
- Is what I'm wearing appropriate?
- Shall I open the door "just as I am?"
- I'm not as clean as I would like to be ...

I let Him come in.
His eyes are so kind.
I sense that He knows me completely, sin and all.
I quickly realize I do not deserve this predestined visit.
"Surprise!" He states softly with a smile.
What is this? He has a gift for me.
Should I open it? He watches intently, expectantly ...
The wrapping is red.
The box is wooden.
I look; there's a heart inside.
He's giving me His heart ...

"I'm so glad I let You in Lord, but You paid way too much for
this gift. When I think of the cost it leaves me speechless.
What could I possibly give You in return?"
My heart you say? My heart?

I surrender all. One box of wood now holds two hearts. It sits before us as we begin to learn more about each other. This gift holds the invitation of a lifetime.

You stay, and we talk into the night. The next thing I know it's morning, and joy has come just as You promised! My heart can hardly believe this will be from everlasting to everlasting!

Before You leave I have to look at the gift once more. Opening the box I see—a miracle! The two hearts have become one; they beat together now with fervent love for each other. And the desire You spoke about, to invite others to receive You and begin life anew, has now become a flame in my soul.

Dear Readers,

Consider the love of Jesus Christ, God's Son, who shed His blood on a wooden tree at Golgotha's hill to pay for our sins, that we might forever be with Him in heaven.

Can you see Him looking for *you* through the centuries of time and coming to *your* heart's door, standing and knocking?

Can you feel your heart beat faster as you begin to open the door?

# An Invitation from Christ

In the beginning God prepared
A place for us to live.
Then came sin—
It entered in; perfection changed to loss.

*But God* sent His only Son
Who died upon the cross,
Then rose again, new life to give,
And now once more
He prepares a place for us to live.

From Genesis to Revelation,
God's heart since creation
Was and is and always will be
For us to be with Him
Throughout eternity.

He waits for you.
For you He longs.
He knows your face
Among the throngs.

He numbers the hairs
Upon your head,
And knows every step
Your feet do tread.

He watches your laughter.
He feels your tears.
His heart's desire—
To calm your fears.

Christ died for your sins
That your guilt would cease.
He shed His blood
To bring you peace.

Who could refuse
His heart of gold?
The price He paid,
The cost, untold.

Take pause,
View Calvary, and you will see
God's Love for you upon that tree.

Loving You, Lord,
As it was meant to be,
Was Your heart for us
From eternity.

You invaded time
As only You can.
The Son of God
Became Son of Man.

Walking the soil of Israel
You called disciples, the gospel to tell.

Many heard Your words.
Others became Your foe.
Nicodemus came by night to listen.
The rich young ruler decided, "No."

It was Your time to speak.
It was our time to hear.
How blessed were those
To whom You drew near.

All the books in the world
Could not hold
The works You did
In days of old.

The years move on
Much faster now
While all heaven waits
For every knee to bow.

With You on Your throne Lord,
Exalted, Most High—
Love will rule and reign
In the sweet by and by.

"Come up hither, Come up here.
Be with Me where I am.
The time is near,
Redemption but a breath away—
Come quickly! Come here!"

"Look, look,
Look unto Me—
See Me dying at Calvary."

"My life, My blood
I freely give.
I freely give that you might live."

"Come and reason," entreats the Lord.
"Behold My cross, My pain.
The price I am paying
Will become your gain."

"Oh, Lord, I receive with humble heart
Your gift of love—forgiveness too.
I choose life forevermore.
I choose You, I choose You."

What joy resounds in heaven above!
Another sinner saved by grace,
Another soul won by God's unyielding love.

The precious blood You shed for me
Flowed freely down Calvary's tree—
Your heart's desire, to set me free.

For the joy set before You,
You endured the cross,
Despising the shame,
Yet paying the cost.

Amazing Grace, how can this be
That You would die for one like me?
Oh joy triumphant, my victory won!
Redeemed by grace through God's own Son.

God's only Son
Sent from above
Endured the cross—
Unfathomable Love.

When I stop and think of the cross You endured,
I scarce can breathe.

The pain, the grief
Heavy on Your shoulders,
The weight of the world You carried.

Your love for sinners shone bright
Amidst the darkness You came to destroy.
The exquisite exchange on display that day—
Deepest of sorrows, the price for joy.

How high the cost?
We will never know.
There is no counting
The debt we owe.

*But God* sent Jesus, His only Son.
Sin's price was forever paid.
The battle over, the victory won,
The hand of judgment was stayed.

Our hearts cry out,
Lord Jesus, to Thee,
"Thank You, thank You
For saving me."

For the rest of our days
Let us never part
From the Love of God,
From Your heart, Lord, from Your heart.

At the cross
Blood flowed freely.
Breath was short, eternity long.

At the cross
Redemption was complete,
And to my heart brought victory's song!

What more could You do,
What more could You give,
That we might live?

Hanging on the cross at Calvary,
Hanging there for all to see—
The indescribable *grace* of God.

# His Invitation to Me

For years I searched
But did not find
That special, perfect place
I carried in my heart and mind.

Where can it be,
This place for me?
Is it on a mountain high?
Is it in a valley low?

But wait, what is this?
A fork in the road ...
Which way should I go?

One road is broad,
Quite busy with crowds,
Noisy, rushing, very loud.

The other is narrow,
Its travelers few.
They walk more slowly.
It's quieter too.

To the right or the left
Not one head turns.
Their eyes straight ahead—
My heart now burns ...

Are they going home?
Do they know the way?
I think I will ask them—
Maybe *this* is the day ...

As I start on the narrow path,
I see a cross—
Then, eyes of love piercing.
All I have gained I now count for loss.

Total surrender,
Total delight—
The clouds are all gone
And the Son shines bright.

My heart leaps for joy!
My eyes now see
That special, perfect place
He prepared for me!

It was there all along
While on earth I did roam—

The road to the cross
Is the road that leads home.

Afterthought:
Salvation's moment—
How precious, how sweet, when time and eternity meet!

Safe am I, Lord,
In Your arms of love,
Safe and secure forevermore.

Hold me steadfast
In the center of Your will
Where I may Thee always adore.

When I see Your face,
I'm humbled by Your grace.
No one can take Your place
In my heart.

And when I hear Your voice,
It bids my heart rejoice.
I have no other choice
But to praise You.

And when I feel Your heart,
Your love to me You impart,
Anew it stirs my heart
To believe. ♥

How near, how dear, You are to me!
Your heart, Your smile, You let me see.
All I can do on bended knee
Is receive, amazed, Your love for me.

When I think of love, I think of You
And how You've proven faithful and true.
Why You chose me, heaven only knows.
Oh, when I think of love, I think of You.

Forever,
For me? Dare I hope?
Can I be from my sins set free?

As I trust on bended knee,
I once was blind but now I see.
With your shed blood comes victory!

Forever Lord,
Yes, it *can* be!
Eternity, for me, with *Thee.*

How can I thank You for all You have done,
For grace that was shown? All battles were won
With arms strong and steadfast, and shoulders to bear
Sins, burdens, joys into Thy care.

Looking ahead, forgetting the past,
Victory in sight—Home at last!

How can this be?
Your love for me,
Eternal and so fair,
Will transport me to heaven's portals
To live with You, forever, there ...

You come to me
In the blink of an eye
The moment I need You,
The minute I cry.

"I will help you"
Was Your promise to me
When I gave You my heart
At Calvary.

Throughout my life
It has always been—
You love me now
As You loved me then.

Unchanging God,
Faithful from on high,
You are my help and my portion.
All is well; my soul breathes a sweet, soft sigh. Selah.

Calvary, Calvary,
Let me never wander far from Thee.
Day by day, as I go my way,
Lord help me to abide with Thee,
Abide with Thee at Calvary.

"1-800-Help 4 Me!"

When I need help
On my Savior I call,
24/7 to my all in all.

He knows my every need,
He knows my every care,
He knows my thoughts far off,
*And* He's *always* there

Smiling and waiting
Just to hear
Words from my lips
As I draw near.

Leaving distractions behind,
I "pick up the phone."
"At last," He says,
"We'll have time alone!"

"Time to enjoy each other's company
And share the day together—"

A preview of coming attractions,
A preview of forever!

Oh happy day
When I shall see
The heavenly home
You prepared for me!

Joy shines in your eyes
As You lead me there,
Arm in arm, with tender care.

"Oh, Lord, I love it!
How did You know?"
Of course.
You've watched me so ...

From childhood through aging
Observing my ways
That changed perspective
With passing days.

From the eyes of a child,
Then hurrying as a teen
To get older quickly
And live my dream.

Next came marriage
And a family to raise.
Memories built
Became "the good old days."

Now a grandparent
With little ones so young—
Me, feeling older.
"Come, let Grandma hold you.
Come rest on my shoulder."

Age is catching up with me,
And limitations are progressing.
My need for You, Lord,
I'm increasingly professing.

The time is near.
The hour is at hand.
It's time to step over
To the Promised Land.

And now here together,
We view Your plan complete.
My thrilling song will always be
Your love over me—how sweet.

When at home I first see You,
Look into Your eyes of infinite love,
My spirit ignites.
I reach to touch
- Your brow that held a crown of thorns
- Your nail scarred hands
- Your sword-pierced side
- Nail prints on Your blessed feet
  That walked this earth bringing good news
- A life gladly given.

I look into Your face
I've waited so long to see.
The only words I can speak—
"For me? All this? For me?"

Oh happy day! ☺

When Jesus washed ✟

My sins away! ♥

# His Invitation to Individuals

"Mary, a Mother's Heart"

Once when He was twelve,
Her son was lost.
For three days she searched,
Her heart and soul tossed.

When He was thirty-three,
She watched Him die at Calvary.

Another three days
Reminiscent of old ...
As He lay in the tomb
Her heart was broken, cold.

But just as when He was a lad of twelve,
She found Him again. Her eyes beheld!
Her son risen, pain gone that she bore,
Her son, now her Savior forevermore!

"The Good Samaritan"

A hurried decision,
A shortcut from Jerusalem to Jericho—
"I wish I'd taken time to think.
Now here I lie, my life on the brink."

Oh, can it be a priest passing by?
I try to call but can only sigh.
Why does he keep walking?
I saw him look this way.
He must have something important to do,
No time to stay ...

At my next glance up, hope was renewed.
A Levite came closer and my helplessness viewed,
But he also passed by on the other side.
How hard to be a victim, then rejected by pride.

I've given up hope now.
There's no one to see.
But, is that a Samaritan
Looking at me?

Not only looking, he's coming this way!
Will I really be saved?
Will I live through this day?

He bound my wounds,
Pouring oil and wine,
Then set me on his beast
And brought me to an inn a little farther down the line.

He cared for me through the night
And on the morrow before he departed,
He asked the innkeeper to continue my care,
Then on his way started.

One more thing I heard him say:
"Whatever the cost, I will repay
When I return again this way."

What a neighbor, what a friend!
He provided for all my needs
Until I was whole again.

Afterthought:
How like Jesus—
Compassion abounding
Conquering love,
The gospel resounding!

"The Woman at the Well"

It was just another day
And I was on my way
To draw water, alone as usual—
No girlfriends to chat with
Or children to watch play.

Within my heart where thoughts are hidden,
I pondered choices that left me guilt-ridden:
Five husbands; the one now, not.
Poor decisions defined my lot.

As I approached Jacob's well,
A wearied traveler was sitting.
I saw He was Jewish
And said it wasn't fitting
To ask for a drink from a Samaritan, a woman.

"If you knew the gift of God
And who is asking for a drink," He said,
"He would have given you living water."
Living water, thirst no more, everlasting life …
My heart He just read!

"Oh, sir, give me this living water!"
"Go, call your husband and come hither."
"I … I have no husband." My heart began to quiver.
He told me He knew, even about the one I'm with now.
I perceive He is a prophet. Should I bow?

"Sir, our fathers worshipped in this mountain
But Ye say Jerusalem."
"The Father seeks those who will worship Him in spirit and
truth."
Spirit and truth; if only I had heard this in my youth …

Anticipation grows, my soul is afire—
"I know that when Messiah comes
He will tell us these things ..."
"I am He."

Now I can hardly breathe from joy;
Right before me, my heart's desire!
The One I searched for all along,
The One to whom I now belong!

Leaving my water pot,
I ran from the well
Back into the city
This news to tell!

I invited the men—
"Come and see this man;
He told me all I ever did—
Is this not the Christ?"

So it came to pass
That many believed what the woman said,
Then, as they listened for themselves to His words,
Were into His kingdom led.

They accepted Him as their Savior,
Responded to His plea.
By the witness of a Samaritan woman,
A city was set free!

"The Women at the Cross"

How could they bear,
The women at the cross,
How could they bear
Seeing You there?

They followed Your footsteps,
Ministered to Your needs.
Now they watched as blood
Formed beads on Your brow,
Then flowed from Your hands, feet and side;
Your garments were parted by soldiers—
Nothing left to hide.

But at the cross they stayed
And, most likely, prayed and prayed.

Maybe they were remembering
The day they each met You
And their lives were never the same.
Each of them found eternal life
When they believed on Your name.

Or the joyful times they watched You play
With children encountered day by day,
People healed from sickness and despair,
Hungry people having lunch by a miracle prepared.

Three blessed years of learning at Your feet,
Salvation's plan was shown many.
Happy were those who believed Your truth.
Enemies? How could there be any?

But as happens in life,
Enemies came; their numbers grew,
Debating, resisting and spreading doubt,
Relentless accusations—
"Who are You?"
"Who are *You?!*"

The more You spoke the truth,
The more their hatred burned
Until it ended at Calvary.
Your love they refused to discern.

The women wondered
How could this be?
How could one look into Your eyes
And not see
Love, kindness and tenderness there?

Even from the cross—
"Father, forgive them;
They know not what they do ..."

But prophecy was being fulfilled
And no one knew, no one knew ...

And so You died.

They took You from the tree,
Laid You in a tomb brand new,
Soldiers once again close by
To guard this Jew.

Then early Sunday morning
Brave women came,
Bringing perfume and ointments
They had prepared—

But found soldiers gone,
An empty grave,
No one there ...

As they stood,
To them You appeared—
Risen! Alive!
Their hearts were cheered!

Joy did come in the morning!
All sorrow left at the tree—
Hearts aflame, O glorious day!
For then, and now, and all eternity.

"The Prodigal Son, The View of a Father's Heart"

Should I or shouldn't I?
They say tough love's the best.
Does he really think going away
Will bring his heart rest?

I can always say no
As well as yes
To his plea for his inheritance.
His plans? I can only guess.

His thoughts are of independence.
His wings he wants to spread.
It breaks my heart to watch him go
And by the world be led.

His mind is set, determined to go.
A far country has stolen his heart.
I cannot speak as I watch him depart ...

Will he ever return home?
Will I again see his face?
My only recourse: to wait and wait
And pray for God's grace.

Away on his journey his substance he spent
On anything and everything, and so the days went.
Enjoying the pleasures of sin for a season,
He had not yet begun to reason.

But it came to pass
A famine covered the land.
He began to be in want
And needed a helping hand.

By God's mercy,
A citizen of the country took him in,
But only to feed the swine.
He could not sit at the man's table;
Not even on husks could he dine.

In the fields with hunger aching
Came memories of food back home, freshly baking.

Coming to himself, he realized his sin.
"I must return to my father's house—
Maybe I can begin again ...
But not as a son—that's asking too much.
I could be as one of our servants; but oh, to feel his touch ..."

As he neared his home, he saw someone running
With arms open wide, laughing, full of joy!
It was the love of a waiting father
Reunited with his youngest boy.

"Father, I have sinned against heaven and you.
Please allow me to be as one of your servants.
Allow me the privilege of waiting on you."

"Oh, my son, a servant you will not be!
You are my son for now and all eternity!
Put on the royal robe, and the ring—
Bring on the fatted calf; let's dance and sing!"

"For when you left, you were lost,
And both of us paid the cost
Of time wasted, time apart.
But now you're found and we can share
Once again each other's heart."

Oh, the mercy, oh, the grace
Of having a Father who waits and waits
And waits ...

# His Invitation to the World

Our time is in Your hands,
Our thoughts are in Your heart,
Your eyes that never sleep watch over us—
Oh, Lord our God, how great Thou art!

When I was but two or three,
I rested upon Jesus' knee.
His smiling eyes will always be
My most favorite memory.

One day I remember clearly,
Mothers brought their children near
For Him to touch and over them pray,
But His disciples said, "Go away."

Jesus quickly responded,
"Do not forbid these little ones.
Let them come unto Me,
For such is the kingdom of heaven."

This is how it will be
When we humble ourselves
Beneath Calvary's tree.

If we come in child-like faith,
His smile we will see,
And our day of redemption
Becomes our fondest memory.

You gave Your all at Calvary
That we might ever be with Thee.

Restoration power
Is available every hour
For those who will ask
At the foot of the cross.

I've pushed so far—
Have I crossed the line?
Have I passed the point of no return?
They say in hell you burn ...

I know I need forgiveness.
There's a strange moving in my heart
Showing me my sin
That has kept us apart.

The quickening my spirit feels
Responds to the gift of Christ revealed.
Now is the time to cross His line,
To choose life and let Jesus be mine.

"Yes, Lord, yes, I come to Thee
Just as I am, to be set free,
Washed in the blood of Calvary's tree."
Thanks be to God for the victory!

Afterthought:
I crossed the line from death to Life
And have become the Bridegroom's wife!

In a little while
He that shall come will come.
In a little while He will not tarry.

In a little while
We shall see His face,
The one who saved us
By His grace.

Oh, precious night in Bethlehem!
To us both great and small,
Born in a lowly manger,
The Savior for us all,

A babe wrapped in swaddling clothes—
God with us, Emanuel,
Born to die—redemption's story
Is now mine to go and tell.

I long to be with You,
Willing right now
To see You in heaven
And before Your throne bow,

But there is much to be done
Still here on earth,
So many souls
Not knowing their worth,

Not knowing the price You paid,
Not realizing the cost
When You left heaven
To die for the lost,

Not knowing that time is of the essence,
Or the unspeakable joy of Your presence
That awaits those who will answer the Savior's call
And find in You their all in all.

"It is written."
"What is written?"
"It is written in the book."

"Every word,
Every deed—
Who is brave enough
To take a look?"

"No, not me!
I'm afraid to see
What is recorded there
About me ..."

"No need to fear
If you come to Jesus,
If you dare to draw near."

"Your story *He* will write,
And by Him you'll be led.
Yes, your name will be there
Written in red." (my thought)

Because of Jesus' blood,
He claims you as His wife.
Forever will your name be seen
In the Lamb's Book of Life!

# Your Reply to His Invitation

One by one we leave this earth
To eternal damnation or by second birth.
These are the choices; stop and consider:
Will you choose wisely or forever be bitter?

Heaven or hell, where is your treasure?
Obeying His call or following your pleasure?
See Christ on the cross, dying for you
With love that is strong, faithful, and true.

Redemption, so costly,
Salvation, so great—
Open wide your heart's door
Before it's too late.

What will you say on judgment day?
What can you say?
"I chose to go my own way,
I chose not to obey."

"But I didn't know …"
That's not really true.
God gave creation
As a witness to you.

And then came the cross.
What more could He give?
He gave His own Son
That you might live.

But you hardened your heart
While His blood flowed red.
Now you find yourself speechless,
Nothing left to be said.

Oh dear readers,
Heed His call.
Come humbly to Christ
As your all in all.

If you give Him your heart
And by His cross stay,
Victory can be yours
On judgment day!

Your vanity,
Your pride,
Your future depends
On what you decide.

Jesus stands waiting,
Loving you so,
Desiring to save you
From hell below.

Must you reject Him?
Must you despise?
How can you refuse
The love from His eyes?

Come to Him quickly
From sin's dread sway.
Salvation awaits you—
Come quickly, today!

The Great I Am descended from His throne
And came to earth to call His own.

The Son of God in a manger lay
A babe born to die, our sins to pay.

He walked this earth inviting all who will,
"Come unto Me, your heart I can fill."

Calvary's cross—oh, the pain He bore
While redeeming our souls to live evermore!

Then came the tomb darkness could not defeat—
On Resurrection morning salvation was complete!

Make haste and come, do not delay.
Your Savior is waiting. *Today* is the day!

The call of the Savior,
His heart revealed.
For the joy set before Him
He endured the cross.

His love for you
Is stronger than death—

Won't you answer His plea?
Repent of your sins
And be set free!

Care to make a reservation
For *your* final destination?
To an inheritance incorruptible and undefiled
That does not fade away?
It can be reserved in heaven for you today!

The cost? *Paid* by Jesus Christ, God's Son.
The battle raged hot, but your victory was won!

Through His death on the cross
The veil of sin was rent, redeeming the lost.

Resurrection morn' completed the plan
Of God's love reaching down to man.

Your part now? To repent and believe—
Salvation is yours when Christ you receive.

He's been waiting for you all along.
Come, join His family in redemption's sweet song!

Once upon eternity
There came to earth
The Son of God,
Incarnate birth.

In wisdom and in grace He grew,
In favor with both God and man,
Redemption clothed in humble flesh,
Our Gift from God, the Great I Am.

He went about doing good.
Many believed He was Messiah.
Others sought to kill Him
And with hearts of stone they called Him liar.

As their fear and hatred grew,
They took Him, nailed Him to a tree,
Not knowing this was God's great plan.
Sin's debt was paid; we were set free!

Ones who loved Him
Took Him, laid Him in a grave.
All hope was gone.
Who was there to save?

Alleluia! The third day, just as He said,
From the grave He broke forth
Alive! No longer dead!

O, glorious morn'
In the garden at the tomb,
His mission was fulfilled
And love was in bloom.

With His disciples and the women
His victory He did share.
Can you imagine those moments?
Can you picture being there?

You can be there to share His joy
If you give to Christ your heart,
He who loves and died for you
And promises never to part.

When to the Savior our hearts we give,
Happily ever after we shall live!

A child is born,
A Son is given ...

No, wait, something is missing—
For *unto us* a child is born,
For *unto us* a Son is given.

Look unto Him and you will see
Reflections of eternity.

A King, born in Bethlehem, lying in a manger—
Have you ever heard anything stranger?

The announcement was by angels to shepherds
As they watched their flocks by night.

A star led wise men from the east and
Guided them with a heavenly light.

A King, taken quickly by night to Egypt
By Joseph and Mary at God's command,
Saved from the slaughter of little ones
By Herod's evil hand.

A King, living in Nazareth?
"Can anything good come out of Nazareth?"
It was once asked.

Still, the child grew and waxed strong in spirit
And God's grace was upon Him.
Before Him lay an eternal task.

A King, coming to be baptized
In the River Jordan?
Did you ever see such a sight?
As He arose out of the water,
The Spirit of God in the form of a dove
Descended from heaven in flight.

And lo, a voice from heaven said:
"This is My beloved Son
In whom I am well pleased."

A King, alone in the wilderness
Forty days and forty nights?
He was foiling Satan's brazen attempts
To make Him give up His position and rights.

A King, walking dusty roads
With nowhere to lay His head?
Pouring out His Father's heart
Everywhere his feet did tread.

Three years of His life He gave
Ministering to the needy and lost.
Then a fickle world rejected Him
And demanded of Him the ultimate cost.

A King, on a cross
For preaching good news?
While the world cursed and reviled Him,
The writing on His cross shone bright—
"Jesus of Nazareth, *King* of the Jews."

A King, in a grave by Golgotha's hill?
"We knew He was just a man."
They thought Him dead behind that stone,
But in truth He had finished the plan.

God's plan that began in Eden's garden
Was by his sovereignty sealed
And ended at a garden tomb
On the first day of the week
When the *King*—yes, the *King* was revealed!

On the shore of Tiberias, a fire of coals,
The aroma of fish and bread in the air
Prepared by the hands of Jesus
With tender, loving care.

The disciples had toiled all night
With not one fish to show.
"Have ye any meat, children?"
The answer back was, "No."

"Cast your net on the right side of the ship and ye shall find."
His words they obeyed.
One hundred and fifty-three great fishes filled the net
And not one got away!

John said to Peter, "It is the Lord ..."
Impetuous Peter jumped into the sea,
This time swimming instead of walking,
With Jesus he wanted to be.

At Christ's request,
Peter drew the net from the shore
And brought the fishes they had caught—
The net? It never tore.

Then from the heart of Jesus
An invitation sublime
To His disciples, and all of us:
"Come and dine, come, dine."

As in times past He took the bread and gave it to them;
Likewise, the fish.
'Twas His third appearance since resurrection
And to be with them was His greatest wish.

Can you feel His love, His desire?
Can you see the coals of fire
With fish and bread prepared for you?
Come and dine with Christ, He who is called faithful and true.

## Benediction

An invitation from the cross,
An earnest plea to all the lost:
"Come unto Me, I paid the cost."

"Your sins are covered by My blood.
Your pain and shame I endured.
When darkness came in like a flood,
Forgiveness reigned—your salvation was secured!"

"Everyone who comes to Me
Comes by way of Calvary's tree
Where eyes are opened and faith sets free.
Come, walk with Me through eternity ..."

## About the Author

This is Faye Stewart's first step into the world of publishing. Discovering the joy of writing later in life, she is grateful for the opportunity to share God's invitation to the world. She lives in Sandston, Virginia, and has three sons and three grandchildren.

Printed in the United States
By Bookmasters